Breaking The Loop of Anxiety

Role of Parents in Overcoming Anxiety in Kids

Louise Castaldi

Independently Published
Printed in the United States of America, First Edition
2020

Louise Castaldi

Table of Content

CHAPTER 1

Introduction

A few years back, I didn't have any way to get success, and I also didn't want to show that to others. In that situation, I was so intolerable. It was difficult for me to take even a single breath, and I got all damp with sweat. I needed to leave. And I wouldn't rest or go out unless I'd ensured the oven was off and the entryways were bolted. Now and again, I do this multiple times. I need to get to the air terminal five hours ahead of schedule. You just never know what may occur.

These are the voices of individuals who have encountered uneasiness. Nervousness is a typical response to life occasions like taking a last test of the year or talking before a group. However, when it turns out to be extremely awkward and makes everyday life challenging to Live, at that point, it's an issue, or even what we call confusion. I know. I've lived with tension for quite a while. My nervousness feels like it's tied in with everything. I stress over numerous things from multiple points of view, and it no doubt impacts my life. I worry about little things that are going to occur or may occur. Furthermore, these worries make it such that I can't generally concentrate on where I am or who I'm with. At times, my heart pounds, I talk quickly, and sort of snap at individuals. My family gets genuinely baffled. At the point when it's downright terrible, I have a knot in my stomach constantly. I can even feel discouraged, and afterward, I simply need to be separated from everyone else.

I think that if I accomplish something, I'll screw it up or something will turn out badly. So, a ton of times, I would just rather stay away. I feel so much better remaining at home and perhaps having a beverage. It turns out nervousness is a typical emotional well-being manifestation.

Nervousness tends to be the fundamental indication of a tension issue, which I have, or social anxiety. Put simply, this is when individuals have a dread of being in broad daylight or meeting new individuals. Again, for those of us with social or generalized anxiety issues, it's tough to live in the manner that we wish to live. A few people have nervousness about extremely explicit things. They fear statues, snakes, arachnids, or something different. These are called fears.

Furthermore, when individuals dodge these things, uneasiness generally remains. At the point when individuals must maintain a strategic distance from their fears, it is a genuine issue. A few people experience nervousness and a horrible pressure issue, or fanatical habitual issue, which can make individuals truly feel defeated with tension. What's more, these conditions of anxiety can be extreme to the point that individuals are in danger of self-destruction, and they use liquor or medications to adapt. Nevertheless, some of the time, they learn to manage it. I'm one of the fortunate ones.

My primary care physician revealed to me how to get treatment that would help, and it did. I now see what my nervousness feels like when it occurs and what can be done. I took in some extraordinary adapting abilities, and even simply naming it keeps it in context. Now and then, my uneasiness can get huge; however, it doesn't appear to keep going as long as it used to. My uneasiness was treatable for the vast majority of situations. You can get your life back to where you need it to be. I realize I got myself back.

CHAPTER 2

What is Anxiety and How It Effect Kids?

We'll look at what anxiety is and how it commonly manifests in children and in adolescence. We'll talk about the common anxiety disorders and how they're diagnosed. And we'll discuss just how prevalent these problems are in the pediatric population.

Further, we'll discuss cognitive behavioral therapy or CBT for childhood anxiety disorders and look at the keys to successfully implementing CBT with children suffering from an anxiety disorder. For example, we'll take a look at how to successfully plan and execute exposures for a child suffering from anxiety. In another talk, we'll discuss the role that anxiety can play in the family, its effect on parents, and strategies for parents to succeed.

Support from parents is important to a child suffering from an anxiety disorder. So, what is anxiety? All things considered, the term is utilized in numerous contexts, yet by and large, it alludes to a person's reaction to any circumstance that they see as a danger to themselves. There are four significant parts to the on-edge reaction, the physiological, enthusiastic, intellectual, and social parts of tension. All these are probably going to become integral factors when a kid encounters an on-edge reaction.

The feeling most ordinarily connected with nervousness is, obviously, that of dread. Dread is often utilized as an equivalent word for uneasiness. Be that as it may, tension can likewise affect different feelings. A kid experiencing tension is likely to feel more outrage and peevishness, maybe as an indication of the battling component in flight or fight.

Additionally, anxiety can impede the experience and the expression of positive emotions such as happiness or enthusiasm. This contributes to anxiety-causing emotions; the emotional life of a child is rather bleak. Some of these are dramatic manifestations of anxiety associated with the physiological symptoms that a child experiences when undergoing anxiety.

Children experiencing anxiety will display acute short-term physiological signs of arousal, such as increased heart rate, rapid breathing, dizziness, and lightheadedness. But they'll also likely experience and display more chronic and ongoing signs of stress and anxiety, such as recurrent abdominal pain, headaches, and various impacts of the loss of sleep. Another effect that anxiety has on an individual is in shaping thought patterns, and this is the cognitive aspect of things. Children experiencing anxiety will likely have many startling situations going through their heads.

What's more, they're probably going to decipher even generally impartial prompts as flagging danger. Kids who encounter nervousness are likely to show a sort of exclusive focus that keeps them centered around whatever it is that sets off the uneasiness.

This isn't a mishap; instead, it's a persistent part of the on-edge reaction. That is valuable when the trigger for tension is a genuine danger. For instance, if I were strolling home from work one day, I may have quite a few musings running through my mind. I might be thinking about something I have to do later that day for work that I have to catch up on, or maybe a friend I'd like to see, or even just what I want to have for supper.

But if I were to notice a truck about to run me over, suddenly all those thoughts would probably be banished from my mind. I'd be focused very narrowly on the immediate threat of the truck, and of course, this is a helpful thought and adaptive response because I'm unlikely to do any of those other things if I've been smashed by a truck.

But for a child suffering from an anxiety disorder, the world might seem full of trucks continually bearing down on them, causing them to experience anxiety all the time, and causing significant interference to their ability to focus their attention on any of the other aspects of development, such as social life or schoolwork. Another cognitive effect of anxiety is the tendency of children experiencing an anxiety disorder to greatly overestimate the probability of risk. Primarily, children will exaggerate the likelihood of the situations that make them anxious, and that are the source of anxiety disorder. So, for example, a child with a fear of going to sleep at night may be fearful because they think that burglars may come to the house.

They might estimate that the probability of that happening is maybe around 50%. Obviously, that's grossly exaggerated, because if that were the case, we'd expect the house to get broken into every other night. And of course, that doesn't happen.

But anxiety will cause the child to overestimate the risk. In fact, not only will the child overestimate the risk of the fear that's the source of anxiety disorder, but anxious children will also overestimate any risk and will consider all negative events to be more likely. So that same child who thinks that it's likely a burglar will come to the house at night is also likely to think that they'll do badly on a test the next day, or that they'll experience some other negative event.

Again, this can contribute to the overall distress and impairment that's caused by a chronic anxiety disorder in a child. Another aspect of anxiety is that of behavior.

Rather, this aspect is that of behavior and the effect that anxiety has on a child's behavioral patterns. First and foremost, anxiety cause avoidance. In other words, you want to stay away from those situations that trigger anxiety. Again, this is a healthy and adaptive aspect of the anxious response to keep us away from things that pose a risk.

But when a child has an anxiety disorder and perceives situations that are not harmful as being threatening, avoidance means that they don't have the opportunity to learn that those situations are actually quite safe. For example, a child who has a fear of dogs will probably avoid any contact with dogs, and they will be robbed of the opportunity to learn that most dogs are actually quite friendly. Or a little girl who has a fear of elevators and walks up the stairs might say to herself,

I'm safe because I took the stairs.

But she won't have the opportunity to learn that she could have been equally safe if she had taken the elevator. Sometimes, avoidance seems like the only way to lower anxiety once it's been triggered. So, for example, a child with persistent worry might engage in a special kind of avoidance. A reassurance-seeking child might pester parents with never-ending questions about their worries to lower the anxiety triggered by those thoughts.

When this happens, the child won't learn that if they don't engage in that kind of avoidance, anxiety is likely to go away on its own. Learning the lesson that anxiety will go away if the child doesn't engage in avoidance is a central part of cognitive-behavioral therapy for anxiety disorders. But what are some of the anxiety disorders or adolescence specific phobias, referring to an exaggerated, irrational fear of any particular situation or stimulus, that are commonly diagnosed in children ? These commonly include fears of animals such as dogs or snakes. They can include other situations, like heights, water, or darkness. Or they could include a fear of needles or just about any other stimulus which can be the focus of a child's phobia. Sometimes, the phobia can easily be related to a specific trigger in the child's history, such as the child who has a fear of dogs and can relate that to the day they had a bad encounter with a dog. But in many other cases, there really isn't a clear trigger for the phobia. And it's usually not helpful to invest too much energy in treatment to trying to identify the trigger that might have been the onset of a child's phobia. One special kind of phobia is termed Separation Anxiety Disorder.

This describes the child who's filled with fear at separation from caretakers, usually parents. Children suffering from separation anxiety disorder can become very anxious even at brief separations, such as being in another room from their parents for a few minutes.

A child with separation anxiety is likely to imagine all kinds of awful things that could happen to them when the parents are away—for example, being kidnapped or getting hurt. Many children's separation anxiety disorder focuses on negative things that could happen to the parents when they're not next to them, for example, getting into a car accident or just disappearing and never coming back.

One other phobia is called social phobia, or sometimes social anxiety disorder. This refers to a kind of extreme and painful shyness that can cause a child to avoid social interaction. The child with social phobia will usually imagine negative outcomes of social interaction, such as making a fool of themselves by saying something silly or making a mistake and being laughed at.

Sometimes, the avoidance will focus on specific kinds of social interaction, such as speaking in front of the class or talking on the phone. But sometimes it will involve a much broader array of interactions that the child avoids leading to almost complete self-isolation. Although children will expend tremendous amounts of effort in ensuring this isolation, the child with a social anxiety disorder doesn't necessarily suffer from a lack of social awareness, or even from a real disinterest in social interaction. In fact, many children with social phobia fervently wish for friendship and company, even as they avoid social interaction because of their fear of feeling bad if they were engaged with another person.

Ga D or generalized anxiety disorder could be characterized as the child has a kind of giant antenna on their head finely tuned to pick up anything there is to possibly worry about. Children with a generalized anxiety disorder will usually move from one worry to another, but never feel relaxed and at ease. One day it might be an item on the news that the child saw saying that cellphones might cause cancer, and then the child could worry for weeks that the people in their family that use cell phones and could get sick and die. Another time the child might overhear parents discussing the family's finances and become tremendously worried that they're all going to be homeless or they won't have enough money.

A child with a generalized anxiety disorder might stay up all night doing and redoing homework because it just doesn't seem good enough, and they're worried that they won't do well in school and about the outcomes that would lead to their life. Children with a generalized anxiety disorder will often engage in a lot of reassurance-seeking behavior and ask their parents questions often to alleviate the distress. They'll often manifest a lot of chronic physical symptoms, such as stomachache and backache. And they'll often have sleep disturbances as well. All these symptoms together lead to a great overlap between generalized anxiety disorder and symptoms of depression. One particular kind of worry is the kind associated with OCD or obsessive-compulsive disorder.

Children with obsessive-compulsive disorder experience unwanted intrusive thoughts or worries that come into their mind, and that they wish they could stop thinking about, but they just can't. And they usually must perform special rituals or repeated behaviors to alleviate the distress caused by those worries.

Typical obsessions include things like thinking about germs, contamination, and sickness, or thinking about awful things that could happen, or even terrible things that the child fears they might do or already have done, such as hurting someone or even killing someone. Parents are often tremendously distressed hearing that their child has these thoughts. But it's important to keep in mind that having an obsessive worry doesn't mean that the child secretly wants to do those awful things, or even that they're particularly likely to do with them.

In fact, it just reflects the child's desire to be good and not to do bad things and the fear that they'll lose control over themselves.

Typical compulsions include things like repeated checking behaviors, such as checking that the doors are locked, or the windows are shut. They might include washing rituals. Sometimes, children will need to do things a specific number of times, such as tapping the table three times or turning the lights on and off four times. Many children also have compulsions related to symmetry, such as the need to line things up on a shelf. So, this can include involving the two sides of the body by touching with their left-hand something that they touched with their right to ensure a kind of inner symmetry.

Panic disorder is characterized by recurrent panic attacks, which are a horrible experience in which it's as if a wire trips in the child's brain and they're just awash in tremendous waves of anxiety accompanied by dramatic physical arousal, heart racing, chest pain, and rapid breathing, and usually including dreadful cognitions such as the thought, this is the end I'm dying, or I'm losing my mind and going insane.

Although panic attacks will almost always subside within around 15 or 20 minutes, many children will come away from experience with one thought: "I'm never going to experience that again." And this can lead to agoraphobia, or the avoidance of situations because of fear of panic symptoms. Taken together, anxiety disorders are probably the most common disorders of childhood, adolescence, and adulthood. Studies have estimated that up to one in three individuals is likely to suffer from an anxiety disorder at some point in their lives. Most adults will recollect that their symptoms had their onset in relatively early childhood.

Maybe as many as 15% of children suffer from an anxiety disorder at a given time. Many of those children, however, will go undiagnosed and untreated for a long time. This is particularly disturbing given information that has garnered considerable support over the years from research into anxiety. We can think of these as the good news and the bad news of childhood anxiety disorders.

The bad news about anxiety is that it doesn't tend to go away if left untreated. Of course, all children will experience transient and age-appropriate fears that will come and go as they develop. But, when an anxiety disorder has taken root in a child's life and has become a persistent source of distress or something that interferes with the child's ability to function in an age-appropriate way, that anxiety disorder is unlikely just to disappear if action isn't taken to help the child to overcome the fear.

This is likely because the ongoing avoidance ensures that the child never has an opportunity to learn that their anxiety is not based in reality. The good news about anxiety is that in the multitude of studies that have looked at treatment for childhood and adolescent anxiety disorders, including studies of both medication and cognitive behavioral therapy, most children who have participated in those studies have improved so that they were either cured of their disorder or experienced significant improvement in their symptoms. Taken together, research shows that anxiety disorders are not likely to go away on their own but will often respond to treatment.

We have a powerful argument for diagnosing and

treating anxiety disorders early.

CHAPTER 3

Impact of Kids' Anxiety on Family System

In this section, we'll look at the way that a child's anxiety might impact the family system and add some strategies for parents to support their child in overcoming anxiety and facing their fears. It's no surprise that parents of children who experience a lot of anxiety become drawn into the child's difficulty because, after all, people are mammals, and young mammals rely on their parents for both protection and reassurance when they experience anxiety. One helpful way to think of the way a child's anxiety might affect the family dynamic is to think of anxiety as blurring the boundaries between parent and child. For example, parents and children occupy different spaces, indicating them being two separate individuals, such as when a parent is at work, and a child is at school, or when a parent sleeps in one room, and a child sleeps in another. But when a child is overly anxious, that space might go away, such as when the child needs to be in the same room as the parent all the time, or when a child wants to sleep in the parent's bed. Parents can ask themselves questions such as, are my actions a reflection of my beliefs and goals as an individual and a parent? Or am I engaging in actions because of the need to alleviate my child's anxiety? For example, parents of children with obsessive-compulsive disorder often find themselves performing compulsive rituals because the child feels anxious.

They may repeatedly check locks on doors because if they don't the child is too afraid to go to sleep. Parents can ask whether their time is managed by themselves or by the child's anxiety disorder, as when a mom needs to take multiple phone calls over the course of the day from an anxious child, or when parents devote endless time to answering reassurance seeking questions.

Even emotions can become entangled between parent and child when a child suffers from an anxiety disorder such that parents feel swept away by the child's anxiety and reflect their own fear back to the child. In one example, a seven-year-old girl was repeatedly taken to the emergency room at night by her parents because of difficulty breathing stemming from anxiety. Although doctors reassured the parents that the child was physically quite healthy, they were unable to withstand the anxiety of seeing their daughter struggling to breathe. And of course, the child's anxiety was tremendously heightened by the experience of being rushed to the hospital at night.

Parents of children with anxiety disorders will often face many dilemmas and ask themselves questions such as "Should I give in to this anxiety? Or should I demand that my child cope better? Is this real anxiety? Or are these just reassurance or attention-seeking behaviors? Is my child just misbehaving?" Or even questions such as "Who am I allowed to tell about my child's anxiety?" In trying to help parents better support their children, it's helpful to address some common misconceptions or traps that parents fall into because of their children's anxiety. Although these misconceptions seem to make sense or appeal to intuition, they can be significant roadblocks to a parent's ability to support their child and overcome anxiety.

One such idea is the thought that anxiety is a dangerous and damaging emotion and that it's the role of parents to protect their children from experiencing anxiety. In fact, not only is this factually incorrect, as anxiety is a normal and healthy phenomenon which children are well equipped to experience, it's also a very problematic message to the child. It's as if parents are saying to the child, you're not able to cope with anxiety, and so I must protect you. The child who comes to believe that they're not able to cope with anxiety is almost assured of continuing to suffer from an anxiety disorder until the attitude changes. Rather, parents should be striving to convey to the child the message that they are able to cope with anxiety. "I'm sure that you can deal with this, and I'm going to help you to overcome this problem." Another parental trap that parents will often fall into is the idea that the child's anxiety needs to be kept secret from anyone outside of the immediate nuclear family.

In fact, many adults who've suffered from anxiety in childhood describe someone outside of the home as being most helpful to them in overcoming their fears. Grandparents, uncles, aunts, neighbors, and counselors can all be tremendous sources of support to both parent and child if they're allowed in, allowed to speak with the child about anxiety, and able to offer help and support. Another misconception that can be a real trap to parenting an anxious child is parents' thinking that if they acknowledge that their child is afraid, they can't ask them to overcome that fear. It's easy to fall into the trap of insisting they're not really afraid, or it's not really frightening. But a child is likely to experience this as a kind of misunderstanding or even abandonment because it's as if we're saying to the child, "I don't believe that you feel what you feel." But the child internally knows that they are afraid. And so, rather than feeling supported, they're likely to feel more alone and less hopeful about overcoming the fear.

It's more helpful to convey to the child the message, "I know that you are afraid, but I believe you can overcome this." This is the stance that we attempt to help parents adopt with regards to their child's anxiety - a stance of support. In other words, combine the idea of acknowledgment and empathy for the child's inner experience of fear and anxiety with a belief and true confidence in the child's ability to withstand anxiety, and some gradual expectations for increased coping. Sometimes, one of the most difficult aspects of parenting a child with an anxiety disorder is identifying and reducing all those ways in which parents are exacerbating the child's anxiety disorder.

This could be through changes to the parents routines and timetables. It could be through providing reassurance, or it could be through doing for the child things that they would otherwise be expected to do for themselves. For example, a child with a social anxiety disorder might be reluctant to speak to someone else, and their parents might become accustomed to speaking for them. Or parents of a child with obsessive-compulsive disorder might feel that they need to engage in rituals, such as washing their hands repeatedly before serving food, because they know that otherwise, the child becomes very agitated and will sometimes even refuse to eat the food that served. This can obviously be very distressing to parents, but we know from a lot of research into childhood anxiety disorders that as long as parents continue to accommodate the child's anxiety disorder, the likelihood of that child overcoming the disorder is quite dramatically reduced. Another difficult aspect of parenting a child with an anxiety disorder is the strain that the child's anxiety can place on the parents' ability to act cooperatively and collaboratively between themselves. Any number of factors can contribute to this difficulty.

For example, parents often have different expectations for the child. One parent might think that not going to Boy Scouts or sleepovers is a sign of disorder, while another parent might feel that that's a legitimate choice on the part of a child, and this could lead to conflict. Sometimes, the different amounts of time that the two parents spend with the child can contribute to their different feelings about the child's situation, such as when one parent only comes home after the child is already in bed, while another one has spent hours reassuring the child or having to accommodate to their anxiety disorder. Sometimes differences in attitudes toward child-rearing can cause conflict, as when one parent is more authoritarian and believes that strict demands should be placed on the child, while another one is more democratic and thinks that the child should be allowed greater leeway and more freedom in choosing how to conduct their own life.

All of these and many other factors can contribute to the difficulty of working together. Sometimes conflict becomes so pronounced that each parent sees the other as actually damaging to the process rather than as helping the child to overcome the fear. But as we've seen, support for an anxious child means combining two quite different attitudes, combining acknowledgment, empathy, and acceptance of the experience with gradual demands for coping. And showing confidence in the child's ability to withstand anxiety.

And so, more often than not, although parents might significantly disagree, they are both standing for an important aspect of support for the child, which is quite necessary for helping the child to overcome anxiety. Recognizing this and coming to see the other parent as reflecting an important aspect of support, rather than as damaging to the process, can greatly help parents in collaborating about the child's anxiety. Increasing communication about the child's anxiety can also be an important tool for increasing cooperation.

Unfortunately, many parents will only talk about their disagreement or about the child's anxiety at the moment when the child is experiencing anxiety and they're under tremendous stress. But this is unlikely to lead to productive communication. Setting aside a special time to talk about the child's anxiety and to discuss strategies for better helping them to overcome the fear can be an important part of increasing cooperation. Additionally, we sometimes encourage parents to trade roles just briefly, sometimes for a few hours or one day, so that the parent who has been in charge of reassurance and empathy takes on the responsibility for helping the child to overcome fear and takes on the role of greater expectations from the child. At the same time, the parent who has been completely responsible for demands and for coping now finds themselves responsible only for reassuring and comforting the child when anxious. This can help parents to see the value in the other parents' point of view, decrease conflict, and increase collaboration. And so, childhood anxiety disorders can place a significant strain on a family system.

But parents are often able to support their child and help them in overcoming fear, growing healthier, and to have the ability to focus more on other adaptive and important aspects of growing up.

CHAPTER 4

The response of Kids in Dealing with Respective Stimuli

We'll discuss the most active ingredient in the treatment of childhood and adolescent anxiety disorders, exposures, and desensitization in this section. By this, we are referring to the process of gradually bringing a child into direct contact with stimuli in the situations that provoke their fear and that they've previously been avoiding. We'll look at some keys to successfully implementing exposures and overcoming some of the obstacles to this treatment. The basic principle of desensitization is easily grasped and, in fact, already familiar to almost all children from a young age. Every child knows things get easier as you do them repeatedly. And that repetition doubles the emotional impact of almost any experience.

For example, a frightening movie is most scary the first time you watch it, but a child knows that if they were to watch the same movie over and over and over again, it would turn from an exciting experience into a rather boring one. To explain to a child how the same principle holds for exposures in the context of cognitive-behavioral therapy, and how it can be applied to helping them overcome their anxiety disorder, we can make use of the wave model of anxiety: The more the wave pushes, the more resistance is met. Ask a child to imagine someone with fear, perhaps a fear of heights, who approaches a balcony and looks out over a high edge. They're likely to experience more and more anxiety.

As they grow more uncomfortable, their mind fills with scary images of themselves falling. They're likely to draw back from the edge in what we term as avoidance. This can lead to a sense of relief and a rapid reduction in anxiety. Although they'll feel better at that point, they won't be any closer to overcoming their anxiety disorder. In fact, next time they approach the edge, they'll feel just as scared, if not even more frightened. But ask a child to imagine what would happen if that individual were to stay looking over the edge and not drawback even though they felt uncomfortable. Their anxiety, which was on the rise, would probably continue to go up until it peaked at some maximum level. This is a good point at which to remind children and parents that although they would be extremely uncomfortable, they wouldn't be at any risk from that anxiety. Nothing catastrophic would happen.

They wouldn't die or faint or lose their mind. They are just uncomfortable. And if they continue to stay there for a few minutes, perhaps 10 or 15 minutes, their anxiety would probably start to go down. And after a while, maybe half an hour, they'd find themselves quite calm. Even though they were still looking over the edge, their brain would just have had enough time to process the information that nothing terrible is happening.

Of course, this would be much harder to do than quick avoidance and its rapid sense of relief. However, by repeating that exercise a few times, they would gradually be able to approach the edge without their anxiety going up all that much. And if they practice this enough, they would soon overcome their fear of heights. This is the principle and the way it's applied. In cognitive-behavioral therapy, there is any number of ways to perform exposures in CBT. But there are some characteristics of successful exposure plans, and together these constitute useful guidelines for planning and executing exposures in treatment. A successful plan will usually ensure that exposures will be gradual, repeated, and prolonged.

Gradual exposure is important to allow the child to only experience a limited amount of anxiety at each step in the process. This is a little bit like climbing a ladder where someone might eventually climb to a great height, but only has to raise their foot about one foot high up in the air at each step to ensure a gradual process that's well suited to a specific child's reaction.

Patients and therapists work together to create an exposure hierarchy. The first steps on the hierarchy must be quite easy and well below the child's maximum tolerance level for anxiety. This is important to ensure success in this early stage of the game. To maintain a child's motivation, it's also important to remind the child that there's still room to make progress and proceed after the initial exposures have been completed. A child who undertakes a tremendously difficult exposure right away might withstand that experience but could come away from it feeling like they can't go any further forward. On the other hand, a child who undertakes only a moderately difficult exposure could come away feeling strengthened and eager to continue the process.

It's useful to ask a child to rate how difficult each step on the exposure hierarchy seems to them, perhaps on a scale of one to 10, or one to 100. But it's important to keep in mind that those ratings, although they're useful for creating the correct sequence of exposures, are only guesses and don't accurately predict how much fear a child will experience. In fact, when anxious, most children will rate almost all steps on the hierarchy as more difficult than they'll turn out to be. This is, in large part, because through the process of continued avoidance, and generalization of that avoidance, the child came to think of many things as difficult when in fact, if they were doing them, they would see that they're not. But it's never useful to try to convince a child that something will be easier than they think. This will only feel to them as if we're belittling their accomplishment. Rather, this is a good opportunity for a child to learn that anxiety cheats them by making things seem even more difficult than they actually are, and for the child to experience that they can actually undertake and withstand challenges that seem really difficult at first. Here's an example of an exposure hierarchy taken from a child with Separation Anxiety Disorder. As you can see, the first steps on the hierarchy are really easy, maybe just a minute in which the parents are in another room, and then maybe a minute with the door closed. Then the parents are in another room, and only after quite a few steps are taken, the child begins to undertake exposures of greater difficulty, such as the parents actually leaving home for a while.

In this example, which is part of the exposure hierarchy from a child with obsessive-compulsive disorder, you can see that the steps on the hierarchy include both exposures to real-life situations and exposures to the kinds of thoughts that make up such an important facet of symptoms in obsessive-compulsive disorder. A second important element in successful exposure treatment is that of repetition. It's almost always a mistake to complete an exposure just once, and then to move ahead to the next step on the hierarchy. Rather, each step should be performed multiple times. This is to ensure that the child is not only able to withstand the anxiety of a given step on the hierarchy but that we've actually turned that event from an anxiety-provoking situation into a kind of nonevent that signals true desensitization. And so, before moving ahead to the next step, the child should be able to rate the previous step as being either quite easy or at least much, much easier than it was before they started.

Exposure treatment is that of duration. Ideally, each exposure will allow time for the child's anxiety to rise, peak, and then subside before any avoidance is undertaken. This will usually take somewhere between 15 and 20 minutes, with the maximum anxiety occurring early in the process. However, very often, children will be unwilling to undertake such a long exposure at the beginning of the process. For example, a child with a fear of darkness might be unwilling to spend 15 or 20 minutes, even in a semi-darkened room. When this is the case, it's a mistake to rigidly insist on continuous exposures of 20 minutes. Rather, the child should be encouraged to do a shorter exposure, sometimes even less than a minute long, in order to allow them to overcome that to see that anxiety isn't as difficult as they thought it might be.

Have them learn to manage their anxiety for short periods of time, and then gradually increase the amount of time. Even though these brief exposures might be theoretically ineffective, they're actually a tremendously important part of the process, allowing the child to ally themselves with the therapist and to begin undertaking exposures to the kinds of situations that they previously have been avoiding. Sometimes their initial exposures will be so brief or easy that they'll represent things that the child might have been doing spontaneously anyway in day to day life. And yet, by defining them as exposure and asking the child to actively engage in them as a way of overcoming anxiety, an important step is being taken. One special kind of exposure is exposure to thoughts and imagination, rather than to real-life situations. These imaginary exposures are useful in two different kinds of situations. One use of imaginary exposure is as a kind of preliminary step to real-life exposure. For example, a child with social anxiety disorder who is planning to undertake a step, such as speaking to a stranger on the street, might find that too difficult to do right away and could benefit from imaginary exposure in which the therapist will guide the child through a kind of imagined scenario of speaking to a stranger on the street and allowing their anxiety to rise in a moderate fashion at that image and then to subside, and as the child becomes desensitized to the idea of speaking to a stranger, they may find themselves more willing to undertake the actual exposure afterward.

Another situation in which imaginary exposures can be helpful is when the child is avoiding their actual thoughts rather than real-life situations. This is often the case in obsessive-compulsive disorder in which children try to avoid intrusive thoughts that cause them distress. And it can also be the case in generalized anxiety disorder in which children try to avoid the persistent worries that intrude on to their mind.

One helpful way of engaging in imaginary exposure is by creating a kind of script or scenario which could be recorded, and then the child could listen to it multiple times over the course of the week, or perhaps writing it in story form and having the child read it over and over again. In one example, a young man with obsessive-compulsive disorder who had a fear of losing the key to his home, because he imagined a burglar finding it and breaking in and hurting his family, felt compelled to engage in prolonged rituals, such as searching for the key to his house whenever he left a room, sometimes for up to 20 minutes at a time, even though the key might have been safely in his pocket.

That young man created a kind of personal horror story, describing how because he stopped doing the ritual he actually did lose his key, and a mean burglar found it and broke into the home and hurt his family and kidnapped him. And although that's a horrible story to listen to the first time, after he listened to it for about half an hour a day over the course of a week or two weeks, he became quite desensitized to the thought, so that he found himself rather bored by it, and his urge to engage in the compulsive rituals was quite dramatically reduced. And so, over the course of cognitive-behavioral therapy for anxiety disorders, children will usually work through a program of gradual, repeated, and prolonged exposures, bringing them into contact with situations that they previously feared and allowing them to become accustomed to them and to disassociate those stimuli from the anxious response.

CHAPTER 5

Treatment of Anxiety in Kids

We'll look at cognitive behavioral therapy for child and adolescent anxiety disorders and how to successfully implement that treatment with children suffering from anxiety. Cognitive-behavioral therapy, or CBT, has garnered considerable support over the years as an effective, evidence-based treatment for childhood anxiety disorders. But what goes into doing CBT? And what are the kinds of things a child is likely to experience throughout the treatment? One helpful way of thinking about what goes on in cognitive behavioral therapy for anxiety is to imagine the child progressing along with two related but also separate tracks on one pathway. One track is that of acquiring skills for better regulating anxiety and better managing anxiety in situations that provoke fear. Think of the child as creating a kind of imaginary toolbox from which to draw when faced with an anxiety-provoking situation. The other track is that of exposure and desensitization. By this, we refer to the process of gradually bringing the child into more and more direct contact with the situations and stimuli that cause fear and that they've been avoiding.

Exposure and desensitization are important part of CBT for anxiety, and we'll talk about them in another section. But what are some of the skills that a child is likely to learn through the course of CBT? Think of the four-component model of anxiety, including the cognitive, behavioral, emotional, and physiological aspects of the anxious response to exposures and desensitization. To impact the behavioral component of anxiety, the other skills will all target the remaining aspects of anxiety. So, the child's toolbox will include three compartments for the emotional, cognitive, and physiological signs of anxiety, several skills targeting the cognitive element of anxiety, and one of the most important therapeutic interventions is that of cognitive restructuring. By this, we mean the process of teaching a child to identify those thoughts that are stemming from the anxiety disorder, and that cause them to experience more anxiety. The child will learn to identify those thoughts and to challenge them by asking questions about the accuracy of the thought or the truthfulness of what their anxiety is telling them. And they'll also learn to formulate alternative cognitions or other thoughts that could compete with those coming from their anxiety disorder. For example, a child with a social anxiety disorder who's having lunch in a school cafeteria might see some children laughing at a nearby table and might automatically have the thought "they're laughing at me."

That thought, stemming from an anxiety disorder, is likely to cause increased distress and anxiety and will increase the probability that the child will avoid the lunchroom in the future. In cognitive restructuring, the child will learn to ask questions, such as, "is it really certain that they're laughing at me?" Or "does every child who's laughing have to be laughing at me?" Even a child with a significant anxiety disorder is likely to recognize that not all laughter is necessarily be directed at them, and could then be encouraged to formulate alternative cognitions, such as they might be laughing at a joke they shared, or maybe they remember something funny that happened earlier. Even if the child isn't yet ready to believe those alternative hypotheses are the correct ones, just by identifying the thought as coming from anxiety and by formulating these possible alternatives, the child is already making progress and will be able to draw from that experience in future anxiety-provoking situations.

In other examples, a child with obsessive-compulsive disorder might have the thought Mommy will die if they don't tap the table four times and can be taught to identify that thought as coming from obsessive-compulsive disorder, and to challenge it with questions such as, "how could that even work," and the child could formulate an alternative such as "that's just my OCD talking." Or a child with panic disorder, who has the thought "I'm dying" when they feel their heart racing could be taught to come up with an alternative, such as "this is just the signs of my panic disorder. It's just anxiety." In treatment, a therapist might ask a child to chart and even journal their anxious thoughts over the course of a week.

They will identify the thoughts coming from anxiety and formulate alternatives. With a younger child, this kind of cognitive restructuring might take the form of play, such as an imaginary boxing match between anxiety and logic. By taking the role of logic, the therapist can model to the child the kind of alternatives that the child will then be able to use when formulating alternatives to their own anxious thoughts. So, for example, a young child might say to the therapist, "you're going to get sick", taking the role of anxiety. And the therapist representing logic might respond with statements such as "I might get sick, but how certain is that to happen" or, "what if I get sick, I'll be uncomfortable for a while and then I'll get better", or even "my parents can take care of me if I get unwell." Another skill that fits into the cognitive compartment of the anxiety toolbox is that of using guided imagery to reduce anxiety. Children, parents, and even therapists are often astounded at the power of imagination in lowering anxiety, and it helps to keep in mind that anxiety is really coming from imagination in the first place. After all, anxiety is all about imagining bad things happening, so it makes sense to combat anxiety in its own natural domain. There are many ways to use the imagination to lower anxiety. A lot of them focus on helping a child to visualize the thought that's provoking anxiety growing more and more distant. Children can do this, for example, by imagining a field perhaps with trees all around and smell of fresh, cut grass in the air and a light breeze, and a blue sky overhead. And then the child can be encouraged to imagine a hot air balloon, gently drifting over.

The child could place their anxious thought in the basket under the hot air balloon and watch as it slowly drifts away from them growing more and more distant until it's only a tiny speck of color in the blue sky. When the hot air balloon disappears completely from view, taking anxiety induced thoughts with it, it's often remarkable how much the anxiety has gone down. Other ways to visualize a thought growing more and more distant could be, for example, a child thinking of their own mind as a kind of crowded train station with people jostling about, and trains pulling in and bringing with them anxious thoughts.

Even a young child can understand that standing on the tracks of a train station and trying to block a train from coming in is not a healthy strategy. But they can also be taught that you don't need to block the train, because if you just wait a minute or two, all trains will eventually pull out of the station and leave taking the anxious thought with them, and they can watch as again the thought goes further and further in the distance, or even just imagining the zoom of a camera lens which could be narrowly focused on whatever is provoking anxiety, but could also drawback to a wider angle. So, the anxious trigger gets smaller and smaller and the child's imagination, other skills, will target the physiological compartment of the anxiety toolbox.

By practicing relaxation exercises, children can both lower their anxiety in the moment and reduce the probability of experiencing heightened anxiety over the course of the day. The two skills most commonly taught in cognitive behavioral therapy for anxiety are progressive muscle relaxation and diaphragmatic breathing.

Progressive muscle relaxation is taught by encouraging a child to consecutively focus on different parts of their body, perhaps starting from the feet. Moving up through the legs, stomach, shoulders, neck, face, arms, and hands to focus on each muscle group in turn and try to relax it so that, by the end of the exercise, the entire body is loose, calm, and relaxed. Diaphragmatic breathing is taught by encouraging your child to inhale slowly through the nose, while allowing the belly to expand to make room for the lungs and the air, and then to exhale slowly through the mouth while allowing the belly to sink back in as the lungs contract.

This kind of diaphragmatic breathing is a powerful signal to the brain that everything is safe. And even one or two minutes of successfully breathing in this way can bring about a dramatic reduction in anxiety. For some children though, relaxation exercises seem to have an almost paradoxical effect, leading to increased anxiety.

Perhaps this is because a child who experiences himself as being at risk might see relaxation as a kind of lowering of the defenses and feel more vulnerable and hence more anxious. Children who feel this way will often be reluctant to engage in relaxation and might become irritable, whiny, or angry when encouraged to do so.

When this happens, it might be most helpful to just choose another tool from the anxiety toolbox. For some children, taking an almost opposite approach, tensing up their whole body, focusing on all those same muscle parts, and holding them tight and taut like a spring for

30 or 60 seconds, and then letting go is a way of achieving relaxation without trying to directly combat the child's tendency to tenseness and rigidity. The emotional compartment of the anxiety toolbox is that least frequently targeted by therapists in cognitive behavioral therapy. However, some helpful skills can fit into this compartment as well.

One helpful principle is that of competing emotions or the idea that it's hard for a child to experience two different feelings at the same time. This is, of course, a problem when anxiety and fear make it hard for a child to experience positive emotions. But it can also be a tool that the child can use. For example, by encouraging a child to actively elicit a feeling other than fear, the experience of fear can be reduced. Some children may be able to do this by making themselves laugh and experiencing mirth or humor.

One little girl chose to do this by changing the scene that she perpetually had in her mind of her father being hurt in a car accident into the set of a movie about a car accident, in which her father was starring, and this amused her so that she was less anxious.

Another child made-up a picture of his mother in the hospital connected to tubes, but then wrote on the picture that the tubes were filled with chocolate milk and made himself laugh.

For some children, however, humor might seem a little out of reach when they're experiencing a lot of anxiety, and other emotions might be more attainable. For example, a child could actively elicit anger, and channel that anger against their anxiety disorder. Young children could make a kind of sock puppet that represents their anxiety disorder, and could get really angry at anxiety and hate it or yell at it. When they feel that anxiety is acting up, as they get angry at their fear, they also feel less afraid. And so, through cognitive-behavioral therapy, children will learn a set of skills that they can draw from when experiencing anxiety, and they'll also undergo a series of exposures to achieve desensitization. Successfully planning and executing exposure and desensitization is the topic of another section.

CHAPTER 6

Tips for Parents to Help Their Kids in Dealing with Anxiety

Here's the usual question I get from parents: "My child is struggling with anxiety. What do I do?" Now you can interchange anxiety with depression, panic attacks, or other things, but the question is always remarkably similar. What do you do if your kid is struggling with anxiety? Number one, I would say, let's make it simple. Listen to them. Stop what you're doing. Put away your phone. Look at your kids in the eye and have a conversation with them - a tough conversation. The problem we have today is many parents do not listen when our kids say that they're struggling. A parent asked me the other day after a talk about how many parents actually don't listen to their kids. And I told him that all I can say is how many emails that I've received in the past 20 or more years, and it's actually in the thousands. Thousands of kids have told their parents they're struggling with things and their parents did nothing. So first, we listen. At the end of listening, you can say that you love your kid, and you will be there to support them in this journey. And then number two, we act. We actually do something.

This is where the problem lies, though. There is no structure we have on how to walk this path to hope, healing, and wholeness. So, we do not know what we must do other than we only know what we've been told. What our churches told us or what we've seen in other people around us. The problem is how do you know what your kid needs? So, my first point on acting is to get assessments done for you to see what you need and what your kids need at this moment. I personally love the concept of body, mind, and soul. These are the three areas I think we need to look at simultaneously. This was talked about back in my university years when I did a phased kinesiology degree.

It is a much talked about a concept in mainstream psychology, and it seems throughout the church world as I often travel in many churches, that their mandate is meeting the physical, emotional, and spiritual needs of the community around them - body, mind, and soul. So, let's look at each of these three categories, and we can kind of look at what we do in each of them.

Now the first is body, and the way to get assessed for

the body is to go to a doctor. Go to a family doctor and get a physical done. Get bloodwork done. See if you might need a sleep specialist. Many of us who struggle with anxiety and depression also struggle with sleep and medicine. I will do another chapter one day on the medicine question, but for now, we just need a balanced approach to medicine, and I would just say simply that if meds are needed, they are okay. You might need a CAT scan or an MRI. I had to go to a neurologist because my anxiety makes me dizzy. I've read books. I've gone to natural paths. You should sleep more. You might get to know a personal trainer to help you exercise better. You might eat better. All of this is under the idea of the body. Now, some of these things are just natural consequences. Your lifestyle might be unsustainable, so take back control of what you can - exercise, sleep, diet, the pace of life, overscheduling attitude, and anything else that you can think of that you can control.

This is where I find a ton of people find help. A guy I know, who was 32 years old, was struggling with self-harm. It's not just a teenage girl phenomenon. And his church said it was a spiritual issue and they were just praying for him weekly. I encouraged him to add to that kind of healing process and go to an actual doctor. Many, many weeks later, he did, and through his bloodwork he found out that he had leukemia.

We need to have the right assessments so that we know what the proper treatment can be. While you are doing the body section, you also look at doing the mind. It's not body or mind or soul; it is body and mind and soul. This should be true whether you are well or whether you're not. For the mind, go see a counselor. A counselor will help your kids get perspective, and maybe a framework for healing.

They might have to look at their pace of life or get some support for their emotions or referrals to a psychiatrist if needed. And the third one -again, body and mind and soul. Now, there are two ways to view this in the mainstream world, the soul might be more soulful or things that fill our soul. For example, when someone goes for a walk, and after you get back, you feel like you've been filled up a little bit. But this could be referring to concepts of well-being and gratitude, volunteering, good relationships, and mindfulness. There's a great app called Calm on the iOS on iPhones and things that focuses on just kind of breathing and calming down. This could be reflection or journaling. I would say even mainstream psychology talks about the importance of faith in these conversations. In our church world, though, I would say we lean towards, as it should be, God. And this might be prayer and Sabbath, like having a day off, and spiritual disciplines.

I do think, and I'll have to do another chapter for this one as well because these topics are just so big, but I do think that often Christians feel that all mental health is spiritually rooted. So, they did not even look at the book. In mind categories, to be really honest, in my 20 plus years as a speaker I actually find the opposite, and I speak 98% of my time in the church world. In all my years as a speaker, I find almost all the answers to mental health have come more from the body and the mind. It's low vitamin D. It's a disease like cancer. It's burnout and breakdown and trauma, things like sexual abuse or physical abuse. It could just be predispositions whereby people have always struggled and feel it's hard to find a way out.

Now don't get me wrong, our faith sustains us through these journeys, but the answer might be something different for people of faith as well. With that being said, I am not saying stop praying. Again, it's the idea of body, mind, and soul. Let me just say that in all these conversations, each of us has different upbringings, different churches, different education, and different experiences, and this has given us our opinions on these things. Often, I find people with medical backgrounds lean towards the body category. Counselors and people like that lean towards the emotional and psychological aspect, to the mind category.

And, too often, people in the Christian church world just assume it's a spiritual battle without any assessment. You cannot just look at someone and tell them what's wrong with them. To go back to our question, what do you do if your kid is struggling with anything - go to a doctor.

See if there's anything physically wrong. Go get some counseling sessions and see if there's anything emotionally wrong. And from a faith perspective, we pray, remembering God is with us in these journeys from the beginning to the end.

CHAPTER 7

How to Spot Anxiety in Kids?

Welcome to this new chapter of survival tips for parents who are raising anxious kids. This book will help parents just like you who are raising anxious kids. And the purpose of this book is to help you understand anxiety and give you concrete ideas, tips, hacks, and anything and everything you can do to help and support your child. So, I thought we'd kick this off, talking about how to spot anxiety, because a lot of times anxiety likes to hide in plain sight. If we can't see what is or is not anxiety, we're not going to know how to approach it with our kids. That is very crucial, because how we approach typical behavior versus how we approach anxiety id not the same. Behavior can be completely different.

And we don't want to coddle and accommodate anxiety, but we want to empower our kids. And we want to give them the tools so they can walk through it. So, I'm going to talk all about the obvious signs and the not so obvious signs of anxiety, so you can spot it.

You have a child and you're not sure if they have anxiety. Are they just a typical child or do you have a child who's diagnosed with an anxiety disorder, and you're not sure sometimes what behaviors are their anxiety and what is normal? This is for all of you, because you need to know how to spot it.

Even if you already know that your child has anxiety, you need to know how to identify it if your child is showing behaviors that might indicate they're having an anxiety issue. So, let's get started. I want to go into the first area that you typically see effects of any kind of mental health issue or any stress impact and that's your basic needs - your sleep, your eating, your ability to function. So, let's break down what that will look like for an anxious child or teenager. When it comes to sleep, I have almost never met a child with anxiety, or teen with anxiety that didn't have a history of some sort of sleep issue, or one they're currently going through. Everything I'm going to say today is just for your education. Obviously, this is not medical advice. Seek the guidance of a qualified professional in your neighborhood. I'm going to be telling you things that might be a red flag. So, poor sleep doesn't equal anxiety. Poor eating doesn't equal anxiety.

I'm not making direct links but a correlation. What I am doing is spotlighting some clues for you to see, because anxiety gives us clues. It says, "hey, look at me, I might be something more than typical behavior," or "hey, look at me, I might be more than just a sleep issue." So, I'm going to spotlight these areas.

And I want you to know that if your child is having some of these struggles, it does not mean they have anxiety. It just means you want to take a closer look. If your child's having sleep issues, that's a great place to take a closer look at what anxiety looks like related to sleep. I'll give you a little synopsis of that. If your child is having a hard time sleeping on their own, that will look different for each one of you.

It might be a no brainer for some of you. You might have a child that is up late at night, terrified, calling you back into their room. "Did you hear that? What was that noise?" You might have a child that has to get up frequently. They need water. They need to go to the bathroom. They want to see what you're doing. And you're just like "come on, just go to sleep." They might be hyperactive during sleep. That one's not as obvious as an anxiety issue, but sometimes that hyperactivity is hyperarousal. So, you can see kids get rambunctious, and bouncy, and feisty around bedtime. Sometimes, ironically, that's an indication of anxiety.

They might be in your bed; they might come to your

bedroom in the middle of the night. They might want to sleep, if they're a teenager, anywhere but their room.

A lot of anxious kids don't feel safe in their room. They might have certain reasons they don't want to admit or talk about. Sometimes there's a closet that bothers them, or a window is bothering them. Normally, they keep that to themselves, but not always. They may want to sleep somewhere in a more communal setting. So, you find these kids on the couches. You find them in the spare bedrooms - anywhere and everywhere other than their room.

You want to look at their sleep issues. Does your child have a hard time falling asleep? Do they have a hard time falling asleep independently? Do they wake up a lot in the middle of the night? Do they have to run into your room? Or do you wake up and find them sleeping somewhere else? Do they need a sibling to sleep with them? Do they need a pet or an animal to sleep with them? Now, some of these things are fine and they're okay. But just because they're okay, such as if you're okay with the dogs sleeping with them, but if your child is showing panic because they need the dog to sleep with them, it doesn't mean that you're going to fix that by having the dog not sleep with them.

But it's, again, a little clue. It's a clue that says my

child might be anxious at night. Now, in this section, we're not going to dive deep into what you do about all these things. We will in other sections, but this section is just about getting your eyes on anxiety. "Hello, anxiety. I see you. I see you everywhere." If you don't know what you're looking at, and you don't know what you're looking for.

Everything else I'm going to be talking about is going to be a moot point because you don't know what is or is not anxiety. So, some other subtle things around sleep that I want to mention before we move on to the next one is that a lot of times these kids will ask questions that maybe don't seem like an anxiety-related question, but they are anxiety in disguise. Sometimes they'll say "when are you going to sleep? What time are you going to sleep? Are you going to go to bed soon? Can you check on me before you go to bed?" Right? And, and most of the time, because those are very specific questions they are indicators of possible anxiety. And the reason why a lot of kids ask those questions is that they don't want to be the last person awake. They want you to guard the door. They want you to check on them because going to sleep is kind of like a mini eight-hour death.

Anxious people lose complete control of their surroundings when they sleep. They don't know what's happening. They're unconscious, and anything and everything can happen. And so, a lot of times kids worry that they may never wake up. They worry that a bad guy will come in. They have no control, and that is why nighttime, bedtime, and sleep tend to be a huge issue for any child with anxiety. And if you have a child with anxiety, and they don't have sleep issues, you just dodged a bullet because nobody wants sleep issues. Sleep issues are the worst because without being able to get a good night's sleep, everything else starts to crumble and anxiety gets bigger. Because when we're weaker because we haven't slept well or eaten well, then everything else becomes more intense and heightened. So, sleep is a big issue. Do you notice any sleep issues with your child? If you want to jot these down that might be a good thing to do as we go forward. And that way, you can kind of look at these and say, "Hmm, what areas do I need to maybe take a second look at" because, even if you know your child has anxiety, a lot of times when people come into my practice they will miss these areas. Now, sleep is an obvious one. We're going to get into some more subtle ones as we move forward.

Sleep let's write that one down. Okay, on to the next one. So, another major biological need and function is eating. A lot of times, eating can be a missed sign of anxiety. I'm going to go into some of the typical things I see with anxious kids who are signal anxiety by diet and by what they eat.

Now, I do want to give a caveat to all of the things I'm talking about and say that I just picked the top eight things that I see most often in my practice. This does not mean there aren't a zillion other things that are signs of anxiety that I'm not including. We can't cover them all, and every child is unique.

So, your child may not present in the way that I'm describing. These are big generalities. And these are just like big spotlights so that you can find the nuances where your child might fit in. I just want to point that out before we move on so that if you're saying, "Hey, you know, my child has a sleep issue, but it's not like what Natasha said, or my child doesn't have any issues with eating and so I guess I could check off anxiety. Now you can't I'm sorry. These are just some pointers. These are just some generalizations and some things that I see that tend to happen. And most of the kids with anxiety don't have all these issues. They have components I've worked with parents that will say, you know what?

I don't know, I don't think my child has anxiety because I mean, they'll jump off the high dive. They like to do really daring things. They water ski, but they're terrified at night. And everyone says you must be a timid anxious person to have anxiety, right? Everybody has different areas where their anxiety impacts them. So, I could be terrified of bad guys, but I could be fine in other situations.

Going scuba diving or waterskiing or playing with snakes. That's not my fear, versus another person who might be terrified of snakes or they might be terrified of heights, but they can go to sleep at night. That's not a big deal. So, anxiety is an incredibly unique thing. And every child is different in how their anxiety presents itself. So, some kids have eating issues and others don't, but when they do, they become very picky about what kind of food they have. A lot of anxious kids have a sensory component. So, they either have a Sensory Processing Disorder (SPD) or they just have some sensory issues and some sensory needs. Not every kid with anxiety has Sensory Processing Disorder.

And not every child with SPD has anxiety. It doesn't work that way. But what I have noticed is that a lot of anxious kids, a huge amount of anxious kids have some sensory things, and that does impact their eating. So, they might be very particular about flavor and taste. They might be nervous about a new flavor, a new bump, a new texture popping up in their mouth unexpectedly. And so, they are cautious eaters, they might only want the mac and cheese from Annie's, or they might want only the chicken nuggets from McDonald's. They can taste the difference. So, if you have a child who is incredibly particular about their food, and then maybe they're super, super picky, and they have only certain foods they can eat, or they don't want their food touching. If their food is touching and they have mixed flavors going together, they might have a huge meltdown depending on their age. And that is because they don't like the unpredictability of their food. And so that comes back to their anxiety. They want everything controlled. They want everything predictable. They don't want any surprises with texture or taste in their mouth or temperature.

That's another one. Now, outside of the sensory issues, other issues revolve around food that I want to touch on. A lot of kids who have anxiety worry about getting sick from their food. And these are kids who are very particular about what is cooked? Did it expire? Where did this come from? What's that black spot there? What's that there? They are scrutinizing their food. So, if you have a child who's looking at expiration dates, who's asking you, "Is this okay to eat?" Then, you need to pay attention to these clues when you have a child who's asking you questions that don't seem typical. I always take data with my kids. All three of my kids have anxiety and OCD. And I'm taking data and so when they ask me questions, there's a part of my brain that is filtering it.

Through my anxiety and OCD filter and saying, "is that an anxiety or OCD question? Could that be an anxiety question?" It's almost happening automatically. And when I get the same questions over and over or a rendition of the same questions, I start to process that with my child. And so, if I'm hearing a lot of questions like - "Does this look cooked?" "Can I eat this?" "Will this make me sick?" "Does this look weird?" "What's this little black dot here?" "Why is this blackness here?" "Why is this hard and this part soft?" - I'm going to start to file that away.

And I'm going to start looking at some food anxiety. The other thing I want to mention when it comes to food, some kids have a fear of choking. And so, this is the last area where I see food being impacted. Just on a general level, there are a million other things, but these are just the main ones I want to highlight. And so, a lot of kids get nervous that they're going to choke on food. These kids might be cutting up their food in tiny, tiny pieces or they want you to cut it up. They might avoid certain foods that they know are choking hazards, such as hot dogs or popcorn, they might over chew. And so, you might see these kids taking an exceedingly long time to eat because they are chewing and chewing and chewing to make sure they can swallow. Now sometimes this goes extreme, where we have kids who can only eat soft foods, and some kids who are only on a liquid diet.

There is an anxiety disorder called ARFID, Avoidant Restrictive Food Intake Disorder. And that's kind of a catch-all diagnosis for sensory issues and these other fears that I was talking about that are all impacting a child's ability to eat. So, if your child is already on a liquid diet, you know that they have ARFID, and hopefully, you're already in treatment. But for those of you that are not dealing with severe issues like ARPIT, I want you to know that anxiety can impact your child's eating. And I want you to understand how so that you can have open eyes and ears to how your child is interacting with their food moving away from eating and sleeping.

We want to move into the body and so, a lot of kids will have physical complaints, somatic complaints, and you want to be aware of what those complaints are that can be related to anxiety. So, stomach issues are by far the number one thing that I see related to anxiety. You always want to rule out medical conditions, but a lot of the time you're not going to find a medical origin, or they might have a medical condition that is either created or exacerbated by anxiety. I'll briefly cover those. Any GI issue, (gastrointestinal issue) could be related to anxiety. Constipation normally starts in toddlerhood. Constipation is a common anxiety issue. Diarrhea is a common anxiety issue. Nausea is known to be best friends with anxiety.

Any upset stomach can be caused by anxiety. Moving from the stomach, there are headaches and migraines. Frequent stress can cause a lot of those issues, and a lot of the panic symptoms can also be very physical. Dry mouth, a lump in their throat, a heart-racing chest pain, feeling fatigued, feeling dizzy, feeling tired. These can all be caused by anxiety. Not fun at all. I always recommend going to the doctor and ruling out anything else. But then, when everything looks good, and you want to look at anxiety as the culprit.

Once you have covered sleep, eating, and their body, we're on to more of the nitty-gritty stuff. Anxiety will greatly impact your child's ability to function. Normally we see the first cracks in the foundation when it comes to going to school. Sometimes the first indication that there's an anxiety issue is school refusal. The first thing I ask after I cover sleep is how school is going, because that's normally not going well. I go how's school going? And if anxiety is really taking its toll on a child, school will be an issue, and a lot of times it's an issue because a child doesn't want to go to school. And it can look like opposition. And some of the reasons why kids are afraid to go to school are because they are either afraid to separate from their parents because their parent makes them feel safe or some reasons listed below are combined.

They're afraid they're going to throw up. And so, they're really worried about throwing up in front of people or getting germs and getting sick from other people. They are worried about performance. Therefore, they might be worried about taking tests, they might be worried about failing. They might be worried about being put on the spot or being self-conscious, or people staring at them, which is social anxiety. I'm going through a zillion different anxiety themes at a rapid pace so that you can get kind of like a potpourri of what types of anxiety issues cause school refusal. That's just the tip of the iceberg. I'm just giving you a sample so you can get the gist of all the many things that can cause a child to not want to go to school. And most kids don't have all of those. They normally have one.

That's really holding them back. A lot of the time, parents will assume the child's being bullied, or they just don't like school, or they have a mean teacher. And they just can't believe that anxiety could be that debilitating. And it can. You don't have to have an external reason why you don't want to go to school. If I am so worried and consumed by my anxious thoughts, that's reason enough. Now along with school refusal, we also see a child who's starting to have an increase in separation anxiety. So, a lot of times those two issues, I would say the fear of throwing up, separation anxiety, and the refusal to go to school are like a trio; they like to hang out together. That doesn't mean you can't have a child with just one. But I'm saying they really all like to hang out together. So if you see an uptick in your child needing to be with you, or maybe this has always happened, and if that's the case, this is not going to be riveting new information for you. But maybe some of you have a child who you suddenly notice becomes your shadow. Wherever you are, your child is there. They're afraid to go upstairs and grab their shoes if no one is up there, or they're afraid to go take a shower by themselves, and they want someone to sit in there, or they're afraid to go brush their teeth, and they want you to be near there.

Suddenly, you're seeing your child need somebody to be near them. They want to go out in the backyard, but they need you to come. That is a clue that your child is having some anxiety issues. It's a clue that you might want to explore why were they able to do that before but they're having a hard time now. No, of course, we wouldn't ask our kids. Why are you having a hard time? What's the matter? And in future episodes, we will go into the best ways to talk to kids so that they're going to open up to you. We don't want to be accusatory. Even if that's not our intention, saying, "why won't you do that?" You know, it comes across that way. So, we want to say "what's the hardest part about, you know, taking a shower, I know it can be scary. What's the hardest part for you?" You want to explore that, and we'll go into that in a different episode. But you want to look at your child and their ability to be independent. And if they are wanting you to go with them, and that's a new behavior, you don't want to cross anxiety off your list, because that might be the reason why your child is having a hard time. Another symptom that is completely missed, a big chunk of the time, is anger. And this one is sad because when we miss this anxiety symptom, it gets mistreated, and it gets approached in a totally wrong way. So, anger and opposition are often signs of anxiety.

Now, not always, we have kids who are just dysregulated. And they don't know how to control their anger and it has nothing to do with anxiety. But many kids don't want to curl up in a ball and shiver and shake nervously. No, they don't.

They don't show their anxiety that way. They show their anxiety by getting irritated and angry and loud and feisty and oppositional and all those behaviors that are not fun to deal with. Right? And the saddest part is when we as parents handle those behaviors as if they're just nasty behaviors. It grows the anxiety, and we see an increase in the behavior. So all those common typical parental approaches that all those well-wishers have told you to do, you know, your child just needs a tougher hand, or you know, you just need stronger boundaries and firmer punishments.

It won't work if it's anxiety. And so, all you're going to do is make your child more anxious, and therefore angrier and who wants that? We want to dive deep and we want to see what just happened. Do you know what happened before this big explosion? Is my child anxious about going to do something? Do I see a lot of anger right before school or before bed or before a test or before a soccer tournament? Am I starting to see some indications that they show anger when they're in a stressful situation?

A lot of times it's subtle. A lot of times there might have been something that happened during the day that they've been fired up over and then they come home. And they share it with everybody. So, anger is actually a big sign that something is not right with that child. And if your child has a history of anxiety, or you're starting to see a pattern in when they get really angry, you want to take a second look and think "Could this be anxiety, because if it is anxiety, I'm not going to address that anger. Through discipline, I'm going to help my child learn how to self-regulate, and I'm going to talk to them and try to get to the core fear that's driving it."

And that'll be a great separate episode that we can dive deeper into because I know a lot of people want help with difficult behaviors. I am also talking about how opposition doesn't have to be a ball of anger, it could just be this defiant opposition of, "I'm not going to do it." And that also can be anxiety in disguise. So like everything else we've been talking about today, it could be a zillion other things and it doesn't have to be anxiety. Sometimes anxiety shows up that way, when you have a child that's full of pride, and they don't want to verbalize or express or communicate to you that they're feeling anxious. A lot of the time, they'll just dig their heels in, and they just will be like, "not going to do it." So you might say, "Come on, we're all going to go out to eat." Maybe you're going to a restaurant that is very triggering for your child, maybe they're afraid they're going to throw up, or maybe they don't like the smells, or maybe they don't want to see other people there. And they're worried their hair doesn't look good, and they have social anxiety.

It's different for every kid. But if your child is not very communicative, they don't like to talk to you about stuff and are not in touch with their own anxiety, they might just double down and be like, "I don't want to go." And you might say, "Well, I'm sorry, young lady, but you don't have a choice in the matter. You're going to go." And your child might say, "I'm not going to go and you can't make me. I hate my life," and boom, you're like, what is going on? All I want to do is take you out for Chinese. I don't know what's happening, and what you're missing.

A lot of the time what we all miss is what's building up in your child's head, all the anxiety that's building up. And so, then we have to back up and work on communication. So that we don't miss those moments where we struggle and suffer through that opposition and nastiness.

And we can just have a conversation about why the restaurant is upsetting so that we can work through it. Even if we know it's anxiety. That's not going to give them a pass. And so that's my message for today in this episode, is, if it's anxiety, come on, you know, just let them be, be nice. It's not that hard at all. It's knowing what your child's triggers are so that you can process it with them, empower them, give them bite-sized challenges so that they can work through it step by step, and give them the tools and skills so they can work through their fears and not avoid them.

We can't do that if we don't know that it's there. So

that is the purpose of understanding why our child is acting that way. The last thing I want to mention is if you have a child who is really liking home, that might be something to take a second look at as well. Because a lot of times, kids who are starting to build up their anxiety, find that home is safe. Home is home base, right? So if I'm here, I'm good. Nothing bad will happen to me. Out there, anything can happen, I might throw up, I might get kidnapped, I might lose you. People might judge me like, whatever my theme is, it's all out there. And not for every kid.

A lot of the time I'm afraid of my shadow and in my house, but if you see your child having some resistance to leaving their house, so going to school is tough, or getting them to go to a restaurant is tough, or getting them to run errands is tough, and it seems like a bigger, more emotional meltdown or opposition than they've done in the past, or what you think is typical for a child. You might want to take a second look at anxiety. Anxiety says don't go out there. It's not safe. There are so many things that can happen to you that are going to be very anxiety-producing if you leave the house. And so a lot of times parents miss this because they think, "well, my child just says they're a homebody, or they're an introvert and they need to recharge. They need a lot of downtime. And that's okay. I'm an introvert and I need a lot of downtime, and I love my home." But if you're starting to see a lot of panic and emotion, when you just say something as simple as, "you know what, I just want to take you out to get some air. So just come with me to the grocery store," and you're getting a lot of panic and negativity. Yeah, then you want to take a second look and see if that might be anxiety-based. So I hope that gave you a good synopsis of some of the main general areas to look at when you're trying to decide if your child is having anxiety or not in all of these different areas of their life. And as I said before, every child is different and so your child is going to be different than the next child and the child after that. Anxiety shows up in different ways for different kids.

So hopefully this gives you some information to file away so that when you're observing your child, maybe for the next week, take some time to just sit back to observe, analyze and ask your child a zillion questions and probe them. We'll talk about this in another episode. But that is a conversation killer. And we don't want to waste any of our special, you know, magic fairy dust on asking our kids too much information and too many questions where they're going to shut down. We're going to work on communication, that's a very important part of anxiety.

But you can quietly observe, play detective, watch your child, watch your child's behaviors in a new light, since you've learned some new things, hopefully, and see what you may or may not have been missing. I miss things with my kids all the time, and I do this for a living. And that's just because I'm so close to it, that sometimes it's hard to get an objective perspective. But when I make a point to say, "I'm going to just be quiet. I'm going to sit back I'm going to just watch this for a minute." Or sometimes I get a little nagging voice in my head.

I don't know that's not a typical reaction. There's something more going on. And I pause, and I watch, and sometimes I will then see the anxiety unfold. Or I'll respond in a different way than that which I wouldn't if it wasn't anxiety. I might say something like, What's the hardest part about that? Or I might say, I know that seems scary to you. And then my child will just crumble and be like, "it is," and "I don't want to go," and I think "oh my gosh, that was anxiety." So, play detective for a week and see how it goes.

CHAPTER 8

Helping Kids with Anxiety, Some Useful Tips

Mom, dad, if you guys are reading, I'm going to gear this today toward the kids so you can have them watch right along or you can just continue to watch to get some ideas about how you might be able to help your own child with anxiety. Did you know that your brain is amazing? It does such cool things all the time. Your brain is in charge of how you think. It's in charge of how you feel. It's in charge of what you do. It's like your brain is like the control center for everything. And it's amazing and awesome. And I'm glad that you have a brain.

Sometimes our brain plays tricks on us, you know, like magic tricks, but the kind that fools you into something that's not real. And one of the tricks our brain plays on us is that it tells us we're in danger when we're not. Now I must tell you something else that's really cool about your brain. Because when your brain thinks you're in danger, it automatically kicks in to take care of you in a really special way. There's a special part of your brain that does this. Different parts of your brain do different things. If it thinks that there's a threat out there.

If it does, the chemicals that activate your fight or flight senses will flow through your system. Those chemicals are called adrenaline. That's why you feel funny when you get nervous or upset. Now, I said earlier, our brain plays tricks on us, and yours does too. In fact, your brain is going to play a little trick on you, to tell you that some things are dangerous even if they're fake. Have you ever been watching TV or a movie and something kind of scary happens and you feel your body reacting? Oh, yeah. Well, are you really in danger? Come on, it's a TV show. But that little part of your brain doesn't know that. And so, you start to feel the adrenaline kick in to take care of you, even though it's not a real threat. You're not really in danger. Sometimes, our brain is tricking us into thinking that we're in danger when we're not. We're at school. Or we're supposed to do something that our mom asked us to do.

"I'm not going to school/doing whatever you asked me." You're not in danger. So, there's some good news, we can trick our brain right back. We're going to trick our brain. There are two things that you can do. That's going to help you feel less nervous, upset, and anxious. And their tricks. Here's how it works. The first one is breathing, because remember, your brain is trying to take care of you. And if it thinks you're in danger even though you're not, it's still going to cause your adrenaline to start up. Breathing tricks that part of your brain into thinking there's no problem. And I said it's a trick but it's actually the truth.

There is no problem. You're not in danger, but we need to trick our brain back into thinking that so here's the way we breathe. Get your parents to do it with you, let's try this together. I want you to do it for just a minute. I want you to breathe in through your nose really deeply, and then I will tell you to and hold it just for a few seconds, and then we're going to breathe out through the mouth, nice and slow, kind of like you're blowing out birthday candles. Make sure to slow it down so that it takes a little longer to breathe out. And then we'll do that again. In through the nose and hold your breath a little bit. Okay, now out through the mouth. Nice and slow.

Blow it all out.

In through the nose again.

Hold just for a few seconds. Okay, now out through the mouth.

Nice and slow. Blow it all out.

In through the nose one more time.

Hold and then out through the mouth nice and slow.

Okay, now Shake it off a little. How did that feel?

You feel kind of good. Maybe a little dizzy. Sometimes people get a little dizzy. That's okay. If you were laughing, you probably didn't get as good of an effect. And I know I'm kind of goofy but notice how that feels. What did we just do? We just tricked your brain.

We tricked your brain into thinking that you're not in danger because you were actually alright, are you not? and that calms down the adrenaline. Because right now you don't feel like you need to fight or run away. Isn't that cool?

Now, I promised you two. So, I'm going to give you another trick that you can do. One of the tricks your brain is playing on you is telling you a lie. And the lie is that you can't handle this, you know, when you're feeling nervous about something. If we were to ask your brain, "what do you think about this," your brain would say, "I can't handle this." Well, it's not true. It's a lie.

So, we're going to trick it right back. Instead, we'll say, "I can handle this." Now when you say it, chin up, have a little confidence. Squint your eyes a little if you need to, and just say, "I can handle this." How did saying that feel? I know you're probably thinking, "what can I handle?" I don't know, I think you can handle anything that comes up in your life. And we want to trick your brain right back into believing that because it's true, and you're a powerful smart kid who can absolutely handle this.

Now, you might not know how you're going to handle it. That's okay. We don't always know how at first, but you got parents who can help you and you got friends and you can keep watching my videos. If that helps. I want you to know that you can do this. Let's trick your brain into believing the truth by saying, "I can handle this." Feels kind of good, huh? Thanks for listening. I hope that's helpful. Parents, if you're still listening, I have to warn you about a common mistake that parents make when they're trying to help their kids with anxiety. And that is, they promise them that certain bad things are not going to happen. If a child is nervous and upset that something might happen to mom while I'm at school, it doesn't help to say, "Oh, honey, don't be ridiculous. Nothing's going to happen."

Because you don't know what if something might happen. Kids' minds usually think "well, what if it does happen, even if you don't believe it can?". If somebody tells you that it's not going to happen? What if it does? That's where we go back to the second hack. Instead of promising them that bad things will happen, reassure them that no matter what happens they can handle it. And we don't have to do this alone. We've got each other to work on this and support each other through it. You can handle it.

CHAPTER 9

Helping Anxious Kids Practical Tips

Childhood anxiety is experiences of worry, and sometimes avoidance of feared situations that are above and beyond what other kids of their age might be experiencing. Some of the symptoms and signs parents may see and children with anxiety are complaining of can be an upset stomach, not feeling well, they may avoid wanting to go to certain places and do certain things. Some children may express their anxiety and hyperactivity so they may be bouncing around the room or they may even experience temper tantrums. Their anxiety may come out in that form as well. The most common types of anxiety in childhood are separation anxiety, social anxiety, generalized anxiety disorder, and school refusal.

If left untreated, childhood anxiety can also affect social relations. The ability to develop meaningful relationships in adulthood can also affect their mental health. They may experience adult symptoms of anxiety. They may experience difficulties with mood - related to how they feel about themselves. For those helping anxious kids, it can be very worrisome to watch a child struggle with anxiety. Thankfully, there are lots that we can do to help kids work through their anxiety, overcome their anxiety, and manage it so that they're able to do the things that they want to do in life. One of the first steps in helping a child cope with their anxiety is an acceptance that there is an anxiety problem. This can be difficult for people who work with children because it's hard to watch kids struggle, and we want them to be successful and we want them to engage in life. But we need to do that at their pace. So, the first step is just to understand what they might be experiencing and what feelings they may be having and empathize with that. Once you've noticed that a child is struggling with anxiety, and you've come to accept that this is part of who they are, the next step is looking at and observing how that anxiety is expressed.

So, paying attention to what they're doing, the words they're saying, what situations the anxiety is coming up is key. What we want to be looking for is patterns in their behavior. Are there certain things or triggers that are common in their expression of their anxiety? Well, in children, more so than older adolescents or adults, we see a lot of physical signs of anxiety and behavioral signs and less ability to articulate what's going on inside to say what it is that's the matter. So, one of the leading signs of anxiety.

One of the leading reasons for referrals from pediatricians, for example, is children with stomach aches, for which there's no physiological cause that can be found. So, stomach aches and headaches are the physical kinds of symptoms children have, as well as restlessness, and some kids are sometimes mistaken for signs of something like hyperactivity and ADHD.

You'll also see other children become withdrawn. Avoidance is the key behavioral sign of anxiety, be it avoidance from general social situations, or refusal to do specific tasks like go to school or try swimming lessons. Once an adult has identified a pattern of anxiety for a child, the next step is looking at how to help the child face those fears.

Children may experience their anxiety as something that's very wrong with them or feel bad about that or about themselves. So it's very important to have a cheerleading approach or a coach approach to work with a child in order to help them feel good about themselves and to help them feel encouraged, but each step that they make towards facing their fears.

It's also important to control your own emotion. Sometimes parents are tempted to try to get through situations by using a loud voice or threatening or forcing, or those kinds of situations. And often that just escalates anxiety. So, when you see the pattern for your child, the next step is to help your child face their fears a step at a time. And often it starts out with very easy activities and might be discussing ahead of time what you're going to do or reading about something you're afraid of in a book, for example, reading books about dogs or insects, if those are the problem, when that's going well then you might get into doing videos about it. And then when that's going well you start to get into short periods of doing the activity. For example, a child who's afraid of dogs after they've read about them and watch them on YouTube, then we might go to a pet store and just watch the dogs. We might be observing the dogs from a place where your child is a little bit challenged, but not too uncomfortable.

And so, if you go in small steps regularly and repeatedly, you can overcome almost any fear. Well, I think that the most important thing for parents to do is to help their children face their fears regularly, step by step. And each day that we face our fear no matter how small the step is, even if it's a baby step, such as I'm afraid of swimming lessons. So today, we just went to the pool, and we didn't even get into a bathing suit.

We sat in the cafeteria. That's a step. And that's much better than saying, "okay, you don't have to" or, "forget it," which is what a lot of us say when we're just frustrated and we have a lot of commitments and, you know, we're just too taxed to push, push, push. But the more we push, the more we're doing our children's service. After being inside the physical building, perhaps the next week, and if a parent has the wherewithal that their child's already expressed a lot of anxiety about swimming lessons, they can start this process long before the lessons actually start.

Next, we're going to get into our bathing suit, and we're going to put our feet in the water. And what I like to do is, I like to say, "we're just going to do that, don't do anything more," because sometimes kids will get there, and after their feet are in the water for 10 or 15 minutes, they'll decide they want to jump in. And I like them to have the perception that they've done more than they even had to, rather than they couldn't do the step. And I mentioned 10 to 15 minutes. That's important. The way that our bodies have evolved in our interference response is that we have an adrenaline rush, we feel like we're on fire for about 10 to 15 minutes when we face something that we really fear. But that adrenaline rush always subsides. So if we stay in the face of that which we fear, say a swimming pool for at least 15 minutes, we will automatically - without doing any other coping behaviors, without having to talk about it, without having to do relaxed breathing, just by physically being there, we're going to get used to being in the swimming pool, we're going to get used to that heavy chlorine smell. And then we would move on and perhaps the next step is to go into the water with a trusted adult, like your parent with, say, a life jacket on. If in swimming lessons, you usually weren't allowed to wear life jackets at that stage. And we're just going to splash around in the water and have fun. And again, being there for 15 minutes is really all it can take. Staying for longer is optional. The more exposure we have and the closer in time that they are to each other, the better. So, doing an exposure week for 10 weeks is great, and we'll probably get any of us over our particular fears. But doing 10 of them - or even five of them - over two or three days is even more likely to be a success.

Because our body and our brains are having less time in between exposures to get back into the old patterns, and we're habituating or getting used to the scary thing very quickly.

Another important step in helping children overcome their fears is to help them think about their worries and their fears in a more realistic way, because of children's lack of experience in the world, and sometimes, their exposure to lots of media about bad things that happen in the world. They can have an unrealistic expectation of those bad things happening in their lives.

Complementary to that is how to work on the worry or the thought part of anxiety. And what works with that area very well is to make sure your child has a realistic understanding of the situation. Give an example of a fear of tornadoes.

Tornadoes can be incredibly destructive. But if you ask your child to start asking family and friends, they'll probably be able to ask every relative and friend they can find and none of them will even have seen a tornado in their whole life, including a grandfather who's 75 years old. So that helps the child put the problem into perspective. If they're asking for reassurance repeatedly, it is probably best to stop giving reassurance, and shift instead to problem-solving. Where you might say something like "well tornadoes are rare, but they're not impossible. I've never experienced a tornado, but if one does come, I hear it."

The sound is like a huge roar, just like a train coming. What's the thing we do in our house when we start to hear that big roar, and what you practice when a tornado comes? The family might do well to have a drill where they practice all running down into the basement, going into the basement stairs, and just sitting there till the noise passes.

When you're learning anything as a child. It's better

to practice not once but quite a few times to really make sure the learning gets firmed up before you move on to the next thing. When helping children talk about their fears and talk about how they can cope with their fears, have children generate some of those solutions themselves. For example, if a child is nervous about changing at school, and they have gym class coming. One way to help them is to sit down with them and talk about what they might be feeling, what their thoughts are about the situation. And what are some possible ideas they have about solving the problem themselves. Kids will often generate a lot of really good ideas that will feel good to them, and it will give them that sense of control and that sense of self-efficacy; that they can also handle problems in the nearest future.

Children with anxiety often used reassurance as a way to help them calm themselves, however, reassurance seeking with adults in their life can actually make the anxiety worse. Try to cut back on the amount of reassurance you're giving your kids, and put that back on to your children in terms of using some of their problem-solving skills. Other ways that they can learn to calm themselves into encouraging children to use their brave behaviors or to try new things is by using rewards. Some of the best rewards are time with the parents, special activities that they like to do, and things that are fun. In thinking about schools and teachers, the schools are positive and favorable environments for kids with anxiety. Most teachers every year will have two or three children in their class who have significant problems with anxiety.

So, most teachers are quite familiar with many of the anxiety situations that come up and they'll have a lot of good strategies from their past experience, and often from their own experiences. Parents, when teachers run into a problem they're not familiar with, they also have specialists to draw on that come to every school. For example, most schools have access to school psychology services, and they can consult with that person about what's best. The key principles we work within talking to teachers is the principle of facing your fear in small steps repeatedly and one step at a time. And very often teachers can work out a strategy for that. Teachers in schools are good at teaching problem-solving skills, which are important to kids and overcoming anxiety.

Funny enough, school is a great place to develop social skills. Children who have social anxiety do experience a lot because many things happen in schools, it just helps them to naturally move along and build their skills and build their confidence.

If a teacher notices that one or two of the children in

the class are really avoiding a lot of situations like playing with others at recess, or something like that, it'd be very good for them to sit down with the other school staff and plan the strategy to deal with these problems. Common strategies that work out really well often pair a youngster up with a buddy who will take them under their wing a little bit and help them engage in activities, creating some simple reward system for approaching rather than avoiding other kids, and pairing up ones that are particularly shy and quiet with other kids who are very positive and supportive. Another issue that's becoming bigger, as it relates to social anxiety in particular, is the issue of screentime.

Children have many, many more opportunities than they used to have for television, computer, iPhone, iPod, handheld games, and for some children with social anxiety and children with other anxiety problems. These things start to crowd out other activities, such as crowding out reading a book, and - extremely worrisome - they can crowd out contact with other children. So, some of the children's social anxiety will refuse or be reluctant to be social, and really prefer to play games on television or on a computer instead. One of the challenges and risks for parents is that the computer or the television can be a fairly good babysitter and keeps the child engaged. And if you don't watch it, it can kind of get out of hand and the child uses it to avoid social interactions. And then when they're missing social interactions, they're missing opportunities to be involved with other children, learn social skills, and build up their confidence.

With most of the families we see, we talk about the parents really taking charge and controlling how much screentime their children have each day, and making sure that the parents are in charge of the devices rather than the children.

Parents play such an important role, far more important than any psychologist helping any child. To overcome their anxiety, and particularly younger kids because it's all about how we structure the environment in our home, do we encourage brave behavior where we face our fears? Or do we have the reinforcement of avoidance behaviors? So, something that parents will do, for example, is talking out loud a lot to each other about their own worries. And they may not have full-blown anxiety disorders, but everyone has daily hassles and stress, right? And so one parent will say to the other parent, "oh, my boss really wants me to go on behalf of the company to that cocktail party, but I won't know anyone and I really don't want to go," and, "Gosh, I don't have anything to wear. I'm just going to tell him that we're going out of town that weekend." And that's an example of modeling avoidance behavior out loud.

Then when our little one really doesn't want to go to a birthday party, and we agree to make up an excuse for that. We're also modeling avoidance behavior, and by keeping them at home, the second we tell the child that they don't have to go do something they don't want to, they instantly feel relieved. And unfortunately, escaping something that's hard becomes paired in the mind's eye with feeling relief, and then it's difficult to go backward and untie those two. And that's what we must do.

We have to pair doing the brave thing with the good, "self-esteem nuggets," as I call them, that children get afterward. And the way that we do that is by taking step by step approaches, instead of all or nothing approaches to dealing with fears. So that the child who doesn't want to go to the sleepover birthday, can have a friend to greet them, and they can go to the first two hours of the birthday party. That's much better than not going at all. Now it's hard to do this as a parent.

And even myself as a child psychologist find it very difficult to see my own child, very distressed, which he certainly has been many times in the past, and I want to give in and I want to rescue him. So, it's helpful in that way to go and talk to someone like a child psychologist because they'll give us the backup and support to be able to do what needs to be done. Facing fears and overcoming anxiety is something that takes time. It's important to practice all the different skills that we've talked about today. And it's important also to have patience with the children that we're working with, and also with ourselves. Well, these tips and ideas can be very helpful.

Sometimes it can be important to seek professional help to common approaches, to helping children deal with anxiety, or looking at medications that can be helpful, or seeking someone who can deliver cognitive behavior therapy. Cognitive behavior therapy is an approach to anxiety that gets a person to look at their thoughts about their worries and their fears, as well as their behaviors of avoidance and also looks at ways that they can learn to calm their body reactions to anxiety. It's important to remember that problems with anxiety aren't solved overnight. However, there are lots of resources out there to help children and adults who care for them to overcome their struggles with anxiety.

CHAPTER 10

Anxiety in Children, How to Know When to Seek Treatment or Medication

This was such a great conversation because we really got granular with the topic of anxiety and phobias as it relates to children. Yes, you explain that they handle anxiety and phobias differently, not only for children but as a subset of people, but also really small children ages 10 and below and also teenagers. Can I explain a little bit about what anxiety looks like among those different age groups?

Well, the first thing that comes to mind is that anxiety does present differently in our younger people. And oftentimes, it has much more of a bodily focus component, especially for younger children. They haven't developed the vocabulary yet to be able to describe their feelings. And so oftentimes, anxiety will present as a stomachache or a headache, or distraction in school. And sometimes you can go down the wrong path diagnostically when you listen to those and take them completely at face value.

Yeah, I was really surprised to hear how common the misdiagnosis was in children who are being brought to a therapist, psychologist, or a psychiatrist for anxiety and ended up getting the wrong diagnosis of ADHD, bipolar disorder, OCD, whatever they are. You talked about some of the tips that parents can use to do the best they can to not get a wrong diagnosis.

What were some of those tips? Well, the first thing is to arm yourself with education. So, you got to make sure you understand when a diagnostic term has been thrown around by a therapist or somebody else that thinks that they know your child.

I've also known that teachers sometimes will diagnose the child and say, "I think your child has ADHD," or whatever term has been thrown around. As a parent, go and do the research and do the research with credible sources. So, get a copy of the DSM - you can buy it. It is expensive, but you can buy the DSM, called the Diagnostic and Statistical Manual of Mental Disorders that providers use to diagnose a mental condition. But also, there are credible websites, for example, the National Institute of Mental Health. They have some of these listings that are actually accurate to the diagnostic manual. So, arm yourself with that knowledge first, and make sure that you ask your provider who is giving you the diagnosis what that means.

Ask them to have a direct dialogue with you. Don't just take it at face value. "Well, what does this mean, in general?" And, "what does it mean in my child? Yeah, what are you seeing in my child that makes you think that they have this diagnosis?" And then the follow up to that is, "how do we address it? What's the treatment plan?" Make sure that you get satisfactory answers from that. You also will talk about phobias. Yeah, what is a phobia? A phobia is an irrational fear of really anything under the sun.

There are different types of phobias. There are contamination phobias, animal phobias, and there's a situational phobia. So, there are really four kinds of different categories of phobias that people can have. Children tend to have a lot of object focused phobias. And often interestingly, also cleanliness, contamination fears. And it's interesting because sometimes phobias are really sort of just developmental. They can be afraid of the monsters under their bed for six months, and that'll go away. But when it doesn't go away, then it's time to seek treatment, especially if it starts to impair the child in their functioning and prevents them from doing the things that they have to do as a child.

What I really enjoyed about this series is that you

didn't just say, "Oh, well, if you think your kid has anxiety, you need to take them to a therapist," which is when I think most parents would expect the answer to be x, especially talking to a doctor. If you gave actionable tips on dialogue with your child, whether they're four years old or 14 years old, what specific questions to ask them to see if they had an anxiety issue or a phobia that required the attention of a professional or if it was something that they could just try to mitigate at home. That's a huge time saver.

That's a money saver. Yes. Huge educational developments. Yeah, so many benefits to that.. And we don't want to over-pathologize anxiety, which we all feel nervous and anxious sometimes. So, this is a quite common human condition. So what I really want people to know is that sometimes there are things that you can do at home, evidence-based strategies of coping that you can teach your children, and if they can manage it on their own, they don't really need therapy. Yeah, and sometimes it's developmental, maybe it's situational. Maybe it's a particular class at school, or a particular person. And once that stressor passes, the anxiety does as well. So, we don't want to make people rush to doctor's offices panicking because they think that their child has a severe anxiety disorder when they maybe don't, even if they are in that space when they recognize this anxiety is getting out of control.

They won't be able to go to school there. They can't sleep. Because they're too anxious. Whatever the symptoms may be, you gave some great advice about finding the right doctor . And my favorite part, enter viewing the doctors. Here's what you had to say about that. Let's take a look. I want to really get it specific here for the parents talking to the therapist, especially when they're still figuring out if it's the right fit or not for their child.. What is, let's say, three to five of the questions they've got to ask?

Okay, I would ask what their experiences treating children with x problem for a particular age range are. "So, what's your experience treating children with an obsessive-compulsive disorder? between the ages of five to seven?" Because some people are amazing at treating individuals of different ranges of ages, but maybe not so much for the age of your child. There is a difference, as we talked about, which is why you're doing the child series on anxiety because with children, anxiety is a different thing than teenagers, adults, and older adults with anxiety. So, you want to know that they've had some experience and are able to describe that to you.

Another important question is to ask them what kind of theoretical modality they work from, is it play therapy? Is it psychodynamic? Is it social learning? Is it cognitive-behavioral, is it a straight behavioral? You want to know where they're going to be taking your child in terms of the techniques that they're teaching them. Psychodynamic therapy is much more insight-oriented, it may not be appropriate for a younger child. Behavioral Therapy is very appropriate for actual children of all ages, but especially younger children when they need that tangible, immediate outcome to know that they're learning something new.

Really great advice. And even if you get the doctor that you think is best, and your teen is on board, or your five-year-old seems to be enjoying the sessions, even then there can be the possibility of a misdiagnosis. What would I advise parents to do if they feel like the diagnosis their child got was wrong?

Well, first they need to talk to the provider who gave the diagnosis, ask them the questions, let them know that you have some concerns that it might not be the appropriate diagnosis, and share what those concerns are. And if you suddenly get a satisfactory answer, and you still have some, just, you know, concerns that maybe it doesn't quite describe your child, the way that you see your child, you should get a second opinion. And I encourage people to be transparent with their primary provider, whoever has been helping them up until this point about that. Yeah, they shouldn't feel like it's a slap in the face if they just want to get a second opinion. It can only help the child more just to get another good professional's eyes on it. I also said it was funny that our director, after we stopped filming the episode was about to mention said, "Hey, thanks for explaining all of those to me because I was a little confused. We went through and you explain it so clearly. SSRIs, which is Selective Serotonin Reuptake Inhibitor." Yeah, better." I'm going to have it?" Yeah. Okay, SSRIs, what's the second one, benzodiazepines, and beta-blockers, and how those are used for anxiety and the treatment of phobias, and how those can be used in children. And the things to look out for? We won't go into every single detail of all three of those, they can watch the series to see that. But what are the big takeaways that parents need to know before medicating their child if that option is on the table?

Well, if that option is on the table, you need to make sure that you have researched the medication class as much as possible, so you can ask informed questions of your prescribing provider. If you are seeing a good psychiatrist or somebody else who has a specialty in dealing with mental health-related medications for children, they should also be able to give you some helpful information to let you know what side effects to watch for, because children's systems are more sensitive than adults', and sometimes are different than adults'. So, the side effects profiles can be quite different. Yeah, so we want to be careful with that. But we also talked about how important sometimes psychotropic medications can be, especially because it helps them receive the therapy a little bit easier, right? It helps them to learn the coping strategies a little bit easier. And in fact, I have known patients who will take beta-blockers or benzodiazepines before exposure to a feared stimulus when they're doing phobia treatment.

What's too scary to even attempt? For example, to get on a plane with the phobia of flying. But maybe if I take a beta-blocker, I'll at least get on the plane and then be able to practice my coping strategies while I'm there. Yeah, that makes sense. I also shared a personal story about my diagnosis with depression and anxiety at the age of nine years old, and how taking medication affected me. Let's take a quick look at that story. I said that at nine years old, I mean, you talk about depression and anxiety. It was off the tribe. I think it was, I don't have anything close to parenthood except for my own experience. But I've been constantly in tears running into the kitchen to grab a knife, just a really tortured nine years old. And I went to a psychiatrist and I was put on Prozac.

And I don't know if they had a pill or not, but back then, they would take Prozac in a syringe. And I remember at the sink, my mom would squirt this liquid in my mouth, and it tasted horrible, blah, blah. But I remember, I mean, probably two or three weeks later, going, Oh, my gosh, I can hear you. Yeah, I can see you. I can wake up I can grab this. I mean, everything seemed clear and how I assumed everyone else was living. Yeah. And so, I only share that story because that was my experience. Yeah. And if you don't want to use medication, don't use medication, right. But if you do use medication, there can be benefits as well as negative side effects, but there can be benefits. And for me, that changes everything. Yeah. And I still feel that way, that medication has helped me and I'm on medication now. And I feel like it does help me.

The biggest lesson I learned from, you and I learned it in our depression and substance abuse series, and then it was reinforced here, was the power of interviewing doctors. Yeah, you permitted the people to do it. Yes. You gave them the questions to ask. And I asked you a question. And I was so shocked at your response. Let's just say, I want them to see this too. So, let's take a look at that interaction right here. What percentage of new parent patients ask you questions before they bring their child in? Less than 2%? And what percentage should be asking questions? 100%? Yeah, yeah, yeah.

Wow, there's no need to hurry. Sure, you want to schedule a session first. Yeah. Sometimes I must engage them first, and then I interview - I basically start the interview. I'm like, "Okay, well tell me a little bit about what's going on. How long has it been going on? How old is your child? What else have you tried?" And then they answer, obviously, because when you ask somebody a question, they answer it, but I'm the one doing all of the asking, which is interesting that they are so ready just to schedule a session without knowing anything that I do. That's a little crazy. I mean, it's a job, right? So, you should feel comfortable interviewing your job applicants. Yeah. And so, when it's a doctor who's going to be treating the mental health of your loved ones, you would think that you want to ask them those questions. Yet only 2% have ever asked me. They just want to get an appointment right away. And I told you, I had all four of my wisdom teeth removed two years ago.

Yes, I don't think I asked that dentist one question, but I asked a lot of questions before I bought my new TV, right? Not that different, right?

Not good. We need to be taking this as seriously as we do our TV.

I get that. You also shared something you haven't shared in the past with the med circle members and I, which is your wellness tips. A wellness program in conjunction with treatment can make everything work better. What is a wellness program? A wellness program is really about a lifestyle. It's a way that you live your life so that you can increase satisfaction, well-being, quality of life, better physical/mental health, and more connectedness with the people that you care about. Yeah. And with that, you don't have to go therapy to have wellness. No, it's things like healthy eating, some kind of exercise regimen, and good sleep habits.

CHAPTER 11

How to Help Your Kid in Dealing With "Separation Anxiety"?

And today I want to talk with you about separation anxiety. Now, I do not like that term. And here's why. That term to me, makes it sound like your child has a problem if they have difficulty being separated from you. So in other words, if your child cries and gets upset, that means he or she does not want to leave your presence. Separation anxiety makes it sound like that's a problem or there's something wrong with your child. That's not the case.

Children, especially young children, I'm talking about those under the age of seven. They are meant to be cared for by people to whom they feel attached. So in other words, your child feels bonded to you and connected to you and the idea that they should just automatically be able to go into someone else's presence and be chill with it is not accurate for a young child; that's not natural. That's not their instinct. So really, when your child is expressing that they are upset at being separated from you, that's really saying, "I'm connected to you and I don't feel fully connected to this other person." And what you want to do is, rather than trying to just calm your child and say, "Oh, it's no big deal, you know, relax." You want to help them bond with that other person. You want them to feel connected because when they feel connected or attached to another person, they are going to feel at ease in that person's presence. They're going to feel safe in their presence. So, I want to talk to you about some specific things that you can do.

Whether your child is going into a school setting, daycare setting, or somebody coming into your home to be a new care provider. Whatever the particulars look like, I want you to be able to help your child feel comfortable in someone else's care.

So the first thing you want to do, and you're probably already doing this, and yet it's worth repeating, is you want to be really conscious about the people with whom you place your child. So, if it's a school setting, you want to feel comfortable with those people. And if you don't get to know them, ask the teacher if you can meet with them privately.

If you are choosing between several daycares, ask other parents, what was their experience, meet again with the providers yourself, give your child a chance to be there with you, and just sort of seeing the energy that they have between the provider and your child. So you really want to be conscious about who you will be choosing to let your child be with, because you really want to feel confident in that relationship, because that's going to be the root of how your child builds confidence and feels confident in that relationship. The thing you want to do when you're making those handovers of your child is you want to do things to calm yourself. So, if you're a parent dropping off a kindergartener, as I did recently, at school, you want to do those things that help you feel calm.

If you're feeling anxious, your child is going to pick up on that. And even if they don't mirror you exactly, they're going to feel your anxiety and you're upset, and it's going to make it hard for them to settle. So that's one of the things you need to focus on early so that you can get yourself calm, confident and excited. Now, that doesn't mean your child's going to be excited about it. But again, your energy is going to have a big influence on how your child interprets this experience. The next thing you want to do is when your child does start to express upset about the pending separation, is you want to empathize with them.

You don't want to try and make it better, so to speak, or get them out of their upset. You just want to empathize and that can be quiet. It can be a lot about your physical presence, your energetic presence. It can also though simply be, "I get you're feeling sad that Mommy's going to work," or, "I know you'd like to be with daddy all day. And right now, it's time to go to school" or, "it's time to go to daycare." You don't have to say much more than that. You want to empathize with their emotions, be with them, accept where they are and don't try and move them through it. They will move through it more easily when you simply accept where they're at. The next thing you want to do, once you have empathized and they're starting to move through some of those emotions, as you want to help your child feel connected, to those new providers, so help them have a sense of comfort.

And so now I want to share some ways that you can do that. What are the actual strategies you can do to help them feel comfortable with a provider? To help your child feel comfortable with a new caregiver or a new teacher, what you need to do is to simply communicate that you are on board, you have great confidence and faith that this is going to be a good fit. It's almost like you're arranging a blind date with your child and this other person. So, you want to be enthusiastic about it. Again, not in a convincing like, "I'm going to try and convince my child to like this person," just to show that you are on board, you're excited, and you think it's going to be great.

So, use that friendliness, that enthusiasm was one of the things you want to do. You want to use the teacher's name or the caregiver's name. You can shake their hands or give them a hug depending on the relationship you have. Basically, it shows again that you're comfortable and this is somebody that you trust. You don't have to say that outright. Your child is going to notice that and say, "oh, okay, mom seems to like this person" or, "dad is okay with this person." Another thing you can do, especially for young children, part of the way they bond and feel connected is when they have similarities to somebody. So, you might point out, "Oh, look, you and Miss. Joan are wearing green today."

"Miss Joan, do you love green? It's Andrew's favorite color." You know, it may seem simple, but it's like, "oh, Joan likes green just like me." It helps them have this sense of "Oh, we have something in common." It piques their curiosity. It could be if you know the person has a dog, and you have dogs, or the person likes trains, and your child likes trains. Whatever it is, start to build that sense of, "Hey, we have something in common."

And again, bottom line, what you're going for is to communicate to your child. I have trust in this person. I am confident that they're going to be the right person to care for you, I trust you in their presence. Since you're not going to be with me right now. A few more things you can do to help ease that time of separation is you want to focus your child's attention on your eventual reunion. So, in our relationships, we are always coming together and coming apart. In those ways of 'we're coming together' to be with each other physically, we're going to be apart physically.

So, you want to point your child's attention to when you reunite again. So that might be as simple as saying, "I'm so excited that this afternoon, when I pick you up, we're going to go to the library and get that book that you just love," or, "we're going to get the next fancy Nancy buck." Whatever it is, point their attention to "we're going to be together again," not, "Oh, we're being separated now," because they know that. So you want to direct their attention to when you get back together again. And then you want to make sure you have a goodbye ritual, something that helps your child still feel connected, even when you're apart. So, for us, we developed a goodbye ritual from a book that we once read called The Kissing Hand. And the story is of a young raccoon, going off to school for the first time, and feeling nervous and not wanting to miss his mother.

And so she tells him the story and kisses the palm of his hand, and says that whenever he needs her, that her kiss will be right there and you can put his hand on his heart or somewhere else and he'll feel the love that his mother has for him through running through him. And so that's where we developed our goodbye ritual. We love that story. And so that's what we did, I would kiss the palm of my daughter's hand. She would give me a kiss to keep with me. And we've had some variations on that. But basically, that was our way to say "okay, goodbye. We're still connected. And I'll see you soon." So you want to have some kind of way to draw the time of your togetherness to a close, so that you can separate and your child can go into what they're going to do. And yet, you can still feel that sense of connection with each other.

The last thing you want to do, is less about doing, and more about what you're going to think to yourself and how you're going to feel. You really want to trust yourself and trust your child. You want to trust those people to whom you are turning your child over to. And just believe that you're all going to get through it. Now, that doesn't mean there aren't going to be bumps. It doesn't mean any of that, it simply means that you put your faith in the idea that we're going to get through this. So even if you feel a little bit shaky, or your child feels a little bit shaky, that you're going to make it through.

And when you cultivate that, again, that's going to be part of what gets communicated nonverbally to your child, that you're confident it's all going to work out. And that helps your child, even if they have bumps. They want to know again, that you're trusting, you're confident, and they will be able to move through those bumps. And part of what they get to cultivate if they do have a bumpy time is, "wow, I made it through." Most of the time, they are going to make it through and they're going to be totally happy within a few minutes of you departing, and they might not even want to be picked up by you later.

They're going to have such a good time. That's what's going to happen most of the time when you give them that space to have their emotional expression. When you communicate confidence ahead of time, and when you keep that trusting energy with you as you do those goodbye rituals and focus their attention on the pending connection that's going to happen when you're together again, they're going to move through it. And they're going to develop resilience from it and confidence in their own abilities to make it through to form new relationships. And it's really going to be a great growth experience for you both. So, I hope this book is helpful and giving you some ideas in ways to ease separation anxiety, and really to ease those transitions when you are going to be separated from your child. And as always, if you have questions or comments, please leave them below as I love to engage in conversation with people. And if you need further support, you can look to my other videos or you can look on my website for additional resources. You can also find the community that I started called the Conscious Mom's Circle. It's on Facebook, and that's a place where I support moms worldwide in their efforts to be a parent free from fear, and really create thriving family lives.

So, thanks so much for your time reading today. And I wish you smooth transitions and a deep connection with your child.

ABOUT THE AUTHOR

Louise Castaldi

Louise Castaldi is an author who specializes in insecurity, anxiety, children's psychology, and social science. In her work, Louise has helped parents to put an end to the negative aspects of anxiety in children, and improve the lives of children and their parents to that is which positive, happy, and healthy. It is Louise's life work to give parents the tools, techniques, and bits of advice they need to improve their relationship with their children.

One of the reasons that Louise started writing on this topic is because she saw children suffering from anxiety and insecurity in her life. Throughout the years, she went through a string of toxic and negative relationships with children that all started from anxiety.

Today it's a little different story from her own. She has overcome her difficulty as a parent of three kids and is enjoying peace and satisfaction in her life. Now, she wants to pass her experience to her readers.

In all of her books, she wants her readers to get lessons and tips through her own experience. Louise provides advice to parents so that they can apply these useful tips in their life to deal with problems. Professional psychologists and counselors who are specialized in kid's anxiety strongly agree with her methods and techniques.